Mamie's HOUSE OF POETRY

Mamie's HOUSE OF POETRY

Inspiring Christian Poems for All Occasions

POETESS MAMIE D. LEE

XULON PRESS

Xulon Press
2301 Lucien Way #415
Maitland, FL 32751
407.339.4217
www.xulonpress.com

© 2022 by Poetess Mamie D. Lee

All rights reserved solely by the author. The author guarantees all contents are original and do not infringe upon the legal rights of any other person or work. No part of this book may be reproduced in any form without the permission of the author.

Due to the changing nature of the Internet, if there are any web addresses, links, or URLs included in this manuscript, these may have been altered and may no longer be accessible. The views and opinions shared in this book belong solely to the author and do not necessarily reflect those of the publisher. The publisher therefore disclaims responsibility for the views or opinions expressed within the work.

Paperback ISBN-13: 978-1-6312-9344-3
Ebook ISBN-13: 978-1-6312-9345-0

Table of Contents

God and Traits He Appreciates
- My Father Above 2
- God Requires Holiness 3
- My Promise To God. 5
- I Read the Word 6
- Failure is in People – Not God's Word 7
- Believe, Receive, and Achieve 8
- Giving Up Wrong for Right 9

Prayer
- Release It In Prayer. 11
- A Prayer for Improvement. 12
- A Prayer For Help 13
- Decrease My Speed 14
- Honor to God and to His Son 15
- Suffering. 16
- Death Had No Hold 17
- Jesus Will Work It Out 19

You
- As An Individual. 20
- You Are a Jewel 21
- Your Smile 22
- I Appreciate You 23

- Denying Yourself.................................... 24
- How I Got Over 25
- How I Got Over – Poem #2 27

Emotion and Love

- Loneliness Hurts.................................... 29
- Broken Vows 30
- Look Ahead 31
- Accepting the Unexpected.......................... 32
- Difficult Emotional Feelings 33
- Feelings.. 34
- Turning From God 35

Woman

- YOU 36
- A Wise Woman..................................... 37
- A Woman Worth Honoring 39
- Godly Women – Keep Working...................... 40
- Women, The Glory of Men 41

Humanity

- Working Together................................... 42
- Our Church... 43
- Pastors Are Human, Too............................ 44
- Stepping Out – Without a Doubt 45
- Thank You, Drivers................................. 47
- What's In a Look?................................... 48
- The Saint's Today 49
- Confessing But Not Possessing...................... 50

Encouragement

- You Are Not Forgotten 51
- Somebody Cares 52
- He's There For You 53
- You've Got A Friend 54
- Don't Give Up 55

Looking Ahead

- Think 56
- Understanding, Wisdom, and Knowledge 57
- Better Ambition 58

Ending

- If Possible 59
- If This is the End 60

Dedication

TO EVERYONE WHO has supported me on this journey of writing a book of Poetry, I appreciate you more than you know. You were never too busy to lend an ear and you unselfishly shared your honest feedback with me. Your role in my life helped perfect this God given gift to write.

To my immediate Family, my Mother and Father in the ministry, Superintendent James & Verleda Watson; to my Greater Joy Church of God in Christ family in Tacoma, WA and to everyone I call family – thank you! To three of the greatest fans ever lived: The late Missionary Florene Gayles and the late Charles and Gayle Canada. I know you are looking down on me today and for that I say, thank you.

My Father Above

My Father ~ who lives above;
is so full of mercy ~ grace and love.
He is a man ~ I greatly admire;
to be just like Him ~ is my earnest desire.

He only stands ~ for that which is right;
and in the eyes of many ~ he is that shining light.
He helps those ~ who are in need;
it is His desire ~ that we all would succeed.

He is never too busy ~ to answer one's call;
He is there to rescue ~ before they utterly fall.
I wish he were my Father
one would say;
But He can become yours,
on this very day.

Just repent from your sins
and invite Him in.
defeat the Devil;
and you will live forever.

God Requires Holiness

Life is a gift
That God gave to you and I;
Holiness is the standby,
we all must follow and live by.

We cannot expect
To merely sit;
With never an effort,
To merit it.

Holiness is required,
even when times are rough.
To God we give our best,
is only just good enough.

We have not the time
To count each loss;
When the bridge is down
Swim all the way across.

Holiness is required,
when life feels vain.
And joy appears to be absent,
even due to pain.

Whatever the Lord
Indeed may ask;
He makes us equal,
and fit for the task.

He simply would not leave
Us alone down here;
And withdraw His love
Of this, I'm sincere.

Strive to be holy
In all your ways;
As you live in these
last and evil days.

My Promise To God

Father, I know not the day nor the hour
When you shall appear,
But since the signs of the time are being fulfilled
I know it is ever so near.

Father, give me
Just what to say,
I promise to be a witness
each and every day.

Lord this is a promise ~ I'm making to you;
Help me to stand and stay true.
Bold for you ~ I want to be;
for Wisdom indeed ~Is what I ask of thee.

I Read the Word

I read God's Word
To see where I stand;
And guilty I was,
of breaking His commands.

All because
I believe what I heard;
But failed to study
God's Holy Word.

I took many chances,
trying to be brave;
If it wasn't for God,
I would be in my grave.

I'm still listening
And reading as I go;
So His will for me,
for certain, I will know.

Failure Is in People – Not God's Word

Never be quick to believe everything people say,
or repeat something you've heard;
For we have nothing to depend on
But God's Holy Word.

Pick up His Word
Read it for yourself;
Stop letting life's power
Lay upon the shelf.

God wants us to rely on His word
Not on what other's heard;
Failure is in people
Not in the Word.

If we follow God's Word
We won't go astray;
It will give you strength
Day after day.

God's Word is all we need in this life
And the one to come;
As long as we have faith
in God's only begotten Son.

Believe, Receive and Achieve

Believe the WORD at all times
So you won't become spiritually blind;
For it's the mind of God
not thinking of mankind.

Receive the WORD with gladness
For the Word of God is right;
It will give you strength to overcome,
any obstacles in sight.

Achieve all you can
While running this race;
But you can't achieve just anything,
without having FAITH.

Faith is believing
Believing is receiving;
and receiving is achieving.

Giving Up Wrong For Right

You must give up the wrong
For that which is right;
To be pleasing and acceptable,
in the Lord's sight.

God already knows
What you are unable to change;
Keep seeking His help,
because to Him, it is not strange.

Trying to live saved
Will only be hard;
If you trust in yourself,
and not in the Lord.

The Lord doesn't have an issue
With what you cannot bear;
Nor does He ignore,
A real sincere prayer.

The Lord never said
Trials you wouldn't go through;
But if you draw near to Him,
He'll draw near to you.

Nobody is perfect,
be it saint or sinner;
But just striving to be,
makes everyone a winner.

God requires the saints
To be victors over sin;
To help those that are lost
And help draw them in.
We must be hearers,
And doers as well.
To keep them from spending,
eternal life in hell.

Release It in Prayer

Whatever it is
That is burdening you today;
Release it to the Lord,
He is listening when you pray.

He's waiting now
To answer your call;
To lift that burden,
so what you do won't fall.

He knows that trouble
Have spilled over in your cup;
He is so willing and able,
and He's there to hold you up.

From this day forward,
In all you are going through;
remember we have a Father,
who has unconditional love for you?

A Prayer for Improvement

Lord, help me to believe your Word
For I know it is true;
When I can't see my way,
I put my trust in you.

Help me to study
A little each day;
Grant me Your wisdom,
Every time I pray.

Help me to believe in you,
and in myself as well;
If I lack in one,
I still would fail.

Lord, I know that you are able
To do all things but fail;
You know I chose Heaven
indeed over hell.

A Prayer for Help

Lord help me to live
By your Word;
And stop going on,
what I heard.

Increase my faith
In you the more;
So doubt can leave,
my heart for sure.

I want to be saved
And do what is right;
Not only on Sunday,
but each day and night.

My spirit is willing
But my flesh is weak;
So Father I pray,
and for your help I seek.

Decrease My Speed

Lord, decrease my speed – this I pray
I want to see need ~ as they come my way.
I'm willing to help ~ anyone I can,
So teach me how – to lend a helping hand.

I'll do whatever – you instruct me to do
Deliverance and power,
comes only through you.

Slow me down,
don't let me move too fast.
If there is any need I can meet;
don't let this moment pass.

I know I can't meet,
All the needs in this land
But allow me to meet;
all those I can.

Honor To God and to His Son

Lord, I thank you for all you have done.
You alone do only what is right.
Thank you Father for giving your Son;
to save my life.

When I was drifting
You didn't let me fall.
Instead you sent your Son,
to help me through it all.

Jesus, thank you for obeying your Father,
concerning my soul.
For through your obedience,
I was forever made whole.

Suffering

Christ Himself suffered
But each time He came through;
So we must follow His example
and be victorious too.

When He was confronted with trials
He didn't give up and spiritually die;
He held on to His Father's promise,
because He knew God could not lie.

The experience of suffering
Is like punishment instead of grace;
That's what makes suffering,
so difficult to face.

Suffering is a trial,
That comes for a reason;
And the hardship that lasts,
is only for a season.

When you reject suffering
You reject the power too;
Because the purpose of suffering,
is to strength both me and you.

Death Had No Hold

While Jesus was doing ~ His Father's will;
So many people – had a plot to kill.
To the high priest ~ He was led;
trying to prove ~ He should be dead.

They had no witness ~ to testify;
One did come forth ~ just to tell a lie.

The priest questioned Jesus,
Because of what he heard;
But our Lord and Saviour;
said not one mumbling word.

He was delivered ~ to pilate by them;
They told pilate ~ CRUCIFY HIM.
What has he done ~ Pilate replied;
but crucify Him ~ is all they cried.

He could have fought back;
But He surrendered instead.
He knew His Father,
could easily raise the dead.

He spoke these words ~ I'll rise again;
as they crucified Him – for bearing our sins.
He gave up the ghost – His life they did take;
during the crucifixion ~ there was an earthquake.

They didn't believe,
Not one word He said;
But three days later
He rose from the dead.

The earth shook again,
the grave opened wide;
Then arose the saints,
who were awaiting inside.

Upon their return,
they noticed the stone;
It was rolled away
our Lord and Savior was gone.

An angel told them ~ He's not here;
yhis caused them ~ to suddenly fear.
Death they could not achieve;
So when Christ got up
they were deceived.

Shocked by what He had done,
Some still doubted
that He was indeed God's son.

We know He is risen,
just as He said;
If He is blessing us daily,
He cannot not be dead!

Jesus Will Work It Out

Whenever your burdens
Seem hard to bear;
It seem like no one care;
seek the Lord in sincere Prayer.

Living a saved life
Is harder than the life of sin;
but it's the only one
That's rewarding at the end.

Your friends will say, "I love you".
And you'll believe its true;
once you get saved
they'll drop you.

The Devil will then,
Bring thoughts to your mind;
but remember only Christ,
can save mankind.

The Devil will make you think
That a sinful life is fine;
but trust God's Word
line by line.

As An Individual

You are an individual,
a person within yourself;
When you are gone,
there's nothing else left.

You are very special,
that's the reason why;
When speaking of a happening
You can say, I.

You are a part of a family,
a portion of society.
You are the other half,
of what makes up the ME.

You are indispensible,
You cannot be replaced;
If there was no you,
there would be no human race.

You are the one I love
And you are the one I need;
You can cause my failure
or you can help me succeed.

The world is populated
by a mass of YOU's;
And you are my concept,
of all I hold as true.

You Are A Jewel

I consider you as a jewel ~ and this I say,
Because you are precious ~ in more than one way.
You gave my life ~ A very special touch
And your friendship to me ~ means so very much.

You are always available ~ when I need a hand.
And your consistent love ~ helps me to stand.
I thank our God ~for the day we met.
And this is a day ~ I will never regret.

I wish you prosperity ~ in all that you do.
Over and above all ~ I really do love you.

Your Smile

Your smile is encouraging and beautiful too.
For I noticed it ~ the first time I met you.
I've had many people ~ to smile at me before
But there's only been a few,
whose were as bright as yours.

Smiles like yours,
so encouraging and true;
It lift's my spirit,
when I'm really going through.

Continue smiling, as you go about your day;
And that very smile
will lift others,
in the same exact way.

I Appreciate You

I appreciate you,
For making me a part;
And the love for others,
you have in your heart.

I appreciate you,
For the life you live;
And for the Word of God
you unselfishly give.

I appreciate your prayers,
When I was down and out;
It showed you cared
and that's without one doubt.

I appreciate a Pastor,
who is a God-fearing Man;
And for his church,
He does all he can.

Denying Yourself

Denying yourself only becomes hard,
when you love yourself,
more than you love the Lord.
There is nothing wrong with loving you,
as long as you remember who is who.

The Lord is the Shepherd
And you are the sheep;
When times get real hard,
you always, will He keep.

Never try to do,
the job of the Lord;
Your Power won't work,
it's just too hard.

Love yourself, but love Him more;
He is the greatest,
and that we know for sure.

How I Got Over

I grew up in a large family,
Where there was more;
Confusion than peace,
being treated differently, I felt like the least.

My parents were drinkers
For as long as I can recall;
It use to upset me,
To see them with alcohol.

Mother could control her liquor,
But my father could;
This cause some situations,
to be often misunderstood.

For my Father was the type of man,
who always wanted to be right;
When mother disagreed
it often led to a fight.

I used to get very angry
With my older sisters and brothers;
They never stepped in but stood by
while our father began to attack our Mother.

I grew up fearing my father,
because He did not play;
One day I asked my mother,
why have a man who treated
you this way?

How I Got Over (Poem #2)

Mother and I were not close
Not because I didn't obey;
It's that I never held my tongue
when I really had something to say.

Mother focused less attention
On us than her friends;
So I started talking,
and seeking out older men.

I wanted to be grown
Before it was my time;
Because my parent's lifestyle,
didn't line up with mine.

Because I talked and acted
On a much higher stage;
I preferred older people
over those of my age.

A friend and I would take,
walks late at night;
Our ages were misjudged,
in other adults sight.

In relationship with older men,
I was blessed the whole while.
They never took advantage of me;
I felt like their child.

They gave me the highest respect
And never pressured me
about having sex.

Even when I was able,
to make ends meet;
That missing motherly love,
made life so incomplete.

I went to visit a church
Where I'd never been before;
A message was delivered
To me from God for sure.

The Preacher told me
Some things about myself;
If I did not change,
I would reap a very swift death.

I left that church
desiring to leave home;
Since Mother and I
were not quite getting along.

I left home in the country
I moved to the city downtown;
Not knowing the area,
I quickly calmed myself down.

Loneliness Hurts

Lord, there are times when I feel
Rejected on every hand;
Because it seems like to me
no one really understand.

Being alone makes me feel
left out and thrown aside;
Because feelings I long to share
I have to hide.

I believe a wedding date for me,
You have already planned;
So strengthen me to wait
for that God-fearing man.

While I'm waiting
Help me to fall in love with you;
So loneliness won't continue
to block my view.

Lord, I know for me
You know what's best;
And it's not you
but the loneliness – I reject.

Broken Vows

When you fail the one you are committed to,
Renewing your vows ~ is the thing to do.
You were not perfect ~ when it was just you,
surely you won't become perfect,
after you say, "I do".

Your marriage may not always be perfect,
but it can be great;
As long as your honesty remains,
betwixt you and your mate.

If you've made numerous of mistakes,
oh well, so what.
Forgiveness will close that door,
and forgetting will keep it shut.

If you are married,
be determined to stay.
When times get really hard,
remember to fast and pray.

Look Ahead

Our marriage will become perfect
And nothing less;
If we enter into it,
giving it our all and our best.

Our love for one another ~ will continue to grow.
If affection is something ~ we constantly show.
Our closeness will remain ~ that we feel.
If we continue to follow;
God's plan and His perfect will.

Our Home will become ~ what it should be.
If I work with you and you work with me.
If we practice looking forward ~ instead of behind,
our future will be great ~ and that we will find.

Accepting the Unexpected

They say, "Life isn't fair",
and it's been proven to be right;
Trying to make a friend,
can be an everyday fight.

Once you meet someone
You begin to learn they are really true;
then you strive to keep others,
from getting between the two of you.

Not that you mean harm,
or you aren't being fair;
It is just that you cherish,
something that is ever so rare.

After sharing all of your faults,
and upon you they still look;
Your feelings got involved,
now you are emotionally hooked.

The thought of losing them,
never entered your mind;
Believing they would never change,
simply had you blind.

Even when it happens,
don't you dare give up;
Disappointments are all a part of
this bitter sweet cup.

Difficult Emotional Feelings

Sometimes my emotions,
Tries to lead me wrong;
But I pray for strength,
To keep holding on.

Sometimes I feel like
Letting my feelings take control.
But they are my post,
So I must patrol.

Your emotions will cause you,
to do something you will regret;
And your conscious won't ever
Let you forget.

With your emotions,
you should never relax;
If you don't stay spiritual
you will become slack.

Don't try to make it,
contribute or exceed;
Just remain Holy,
and You will succeed.

Feelings

Feelings are nothing to be play with,
Because they can be easily hurt;
Some may treat other's feelings,
as if they were nothing but dirt.

Feelings will show
Whether you love or don't care;
They are something you hold on to
and long to share.

Feelings some will hide
Behind a cherry smile;
While hurting inside
all the while.

Love is a feeling,
We must strive to show.
To help one another,
as they positively grow.

Turning From God

Once in my life,
not too long ago,
I was going to church and doing just fine;
I met some people and allowed my feelings,
to get way out of line.

When I'm doing good and looking up
instead of looking down;
The devil sends uncaring people;
to pull me to the ground.

Within my mind – I began to feel
I'm a nobody;
But I must convince myself,
God made me – somebody.

When helping others,
You might get hurt;
For this is how,
that o'l devil works.

Don't allow your feelings
To go over the line;
Don't turn from God,
because of mankind.

YOU

You are worthy to be honored today
This is the reason why;
You are always available when needed
And always willing to try.

You are a great inspiration
Whenever you talk;
Because the words you speak,
lines up with your walk.

You are a Woman of God
Whose priorities are straight;
This makes you honorable,
and it makes you great.

You are faithful at lifting
Those who are down and out.
Telling them to believe,
and never walk in doubt.

You warm the hearts of many,
each time you smile;
Having you as a honoree today,
makes honoring very worthwhile.

A Wise Woman

A wise woman is one
Who reverences the Lord;
And knows' He is God
When times get hard.

The Word of God
She strive to obey;
She works with her husband
In every possible way.

She always acknowledge him
As being he head;
His power of authority
She does not dread.

She teaches her children
Things that are right;
She encourages them to pray
Both day and night.

She forgives others
Along the way;
And ask to be forgiven
Each time she prays.

She prays for strength,
when she is weak;
And that which she knows,
is all she will speak.

She never pretend
During any task;
When uncertain
She will just ask.

She contributes to needs,
whenever she can;
Consider it herself,
needing a helping hand.

She never does
What she feel;
unless it's in
God's perfect will.

For in His will,
lies her plans;
So her family and hom
Will always stand.

A Woman Worth Honoring

A woman worth honoring
Is a Woman of the Lord;
Because she is there for you,
when times get hard.

She is indeed faithful
At telling you what is right;
And the Word of God,
she doesn't take light.

She considers others
Whenever she prays;
She will only do,
what she hear the Lord say.

She is true and honest
In all that she do;
This Woman tonight,
is none other than YOU.

Godly Women – Keep Working

Women the hour is coming
And it's getting late
No time to stop
No time to procrastinate.

God has saved
Both you and I;
We must keep working
To the day we die.

We cannot let stress
Slow us down;
Nor can we let people
Turn us around.

God is depending
On me and you,
To live Holy
And be a witness too.

He has place His Spirit
Deep within
He gave us His power
To draw the souls in.

To win those souls,
Who have gone astray;
We must keep working,
while it is day.

Women, The Glory of Men

When God created you and I,
He made us the glory ~ of a man's eye.
Thankful unto Him ~ we should be,
For considering us ~ ever so worthy.

He could have chosen,
an angel from above;
But He chose you and I,
Through His goodness and unconditional love.

He could have made us the foot,
Since man is the head.
But the position of glory
Is where He placed us instead.

Be proud as you walk
Through the streets of this land;
Knowing you are a child of God,
And you are the glory of the man.

Working Together

If we expect ~ to make it above,
We must first work together ~ in unity and with love.
For then and only then ~ sin we will defeat,
Because togetherness makes ~ the whole church complete.

We've been made Sister's and Brother's
And God wants us ~ to help one another.

It takes us all ~and this is why,
Not one coal alone ~ can start the fire.

We have the spark ~ and the draft too.
It is the spirit of God ~ in me and in you.

Let us work together ~ and the fire will burn,
Destroying the sin – is our main concern.

Let's catch on fire ~ for God likes coals,
We can work together – and win some souls.

Our Church

If we love our church – just as we say,
Then let us support it ~ in more than one way.

If Holy is the way ~ and we confess to live,
Let us do better – even when we give.

We sow with our money,
and our time;
To prevent unnecessary stress,
that sits upon our Pastor's mind.

Our Pastor needs us ~ let us lend a hand,
We must help our church – in every way we can.

He is working hard ~ and that is not good,
All because we don't do – just as we should.

He has a job ~ and family too
Responsibilities daily ~ Just like me and you.
Helping other ~ He won't neglect
The House He Pastors ~ He never forgets.

He is thankful when Friends and Guest ~ stop by
He is depending on ~ God, you and I.

Let us keep our Pastor,
lifted in prayer;
forever show our church,
we do love and we do care.

Pastors Are Human Too

Pastors are not perfect ~ and here's the reason why.
They all are human ~ just like you and I.
They can bear their burdens – and the burdens of all
And being all so human ~ they are subject to fall.

It is not for us to say ~ preaching is not their call;
They can make mistakes, mishaps or they can simply fall.
They are in need of prayer ~ just like you and I.
For they have good days ~ and those days quickly pass by.

We should not criticize them ~ and I'll tell you why,
They have real feelings ~ just like you and I.
Their job is not as easy ~ as it may appear.
They are willing to help us ~ even through our worst fears.

They are the Shepherds ~ we are the sheep.
They are up working ~ while we are fast asleep.
They are Praying ~ when we are talking.
They are constantly running ~ while we are barely walking.

When we disagree ~ with something they do or say,
What we should do
is watch and Pray.

Stepping Out – Without A Doubt

Now is the time, you are required to move,
Your Faith in God – This will prove.
When becoming an author, patience is a must,
totally in God ~ you have to trust.

Friends are great ~ be it many or few,
For you will need ~ their support too.
By word of mouth, has proven to be;
the best advertising – or publicity.

Those who promote Author's
must do it well,
To help them move forward,
so their material can sell.

Wisdom and knowledge,
the buyers should gain;
With all they have,
they for sure must obtain.

When a real author is saved
God they truly seek;
they will write what they hear
when only He speak.

If this is done,
without taking a chance,
God will grant a speedy advance.

As your business begin to grow
Here is something you should know.
It doesn't matter if you are new,
real authors had a beginning too.

The Lord gives,
the devil takes;
Man can't do it
so make no mistake.

If you stay before the Lord
ever so humble.
Your business will never fall;
Nor will it crumble.

Thank You Drivers

Thank you drivers,
For driving the bus;
Your public service daily,
Has helped so many of us.

If it wasn't for what you do,
We couldn't go far;
We either can't drive,
Or we have no car.

Your humble service,
Day after day;
Is quite a blessing to us
In a very unique way.

May your Holidays be blessed
And your New Years too;
May what you so desire the most,
is granted unto you.

We wish you success
In all that you do;
From the depths of our hearts,
we say, THANK YOU!

What's In a Look?

Looks can be deceiving
Here's the reason why;
A persons eyes may smile at you
But their eyes can tell a lie.

Every face that wears a smile
May not be worn by a friend.
A frozen lake can look so safe
But the ice can be so thin.

A blue sky looks so lovely
Without a cloud in sight.
But beware of its looks,
It might storm before the night.

A Rose can look so beautiful
And silky to the touch.
But picking it in haste,
Its thorns has a painful thrust.

A river can look so peaceful
As it goes flowing by.
But how many undercurrents,
has caused one to die?

The Saint's Today

We the saints of today
Are going astray;
We are resembling the world
In more than one way.

Some of us are determined
To do what is right;
And we strive every day
To be a light.

Others of us are so busy
Trying to be the head;
Until we miss God's way
And follow our's instead.

Many of us are good
At keeping up with mess;
We talk the most
And by far, do less.

Few of us will remain faithful
And never think twice;
When doing or giving
Because a real sacrifice.

All of us say, "I love the Lord"
And our Pastor's too;
But the number of workers
Are so very few.

Confessing but Not Possessing

Lord, some of us claimed to be saved,
and this we faithfully confess.
But, the fruits we are bearing;
are those that pertaineth to the flesh.

Some of us at times will say
We have your spirit deep within
But are only loving on certain ones
Or, those we call our friend.

Some of us are quick to quote the Word,
to those who are acting out of line.
But we are guilty of the same thing,
most of the time.

Lord, perfection won't be accomplished,
until we meet with you.
But keep us mindful that we're charged
for what we know and don't do.

Getting our lives right with you,
isn't a might but a must.
So Lord work both your will,
and your righteousness in us.

Help us not to confess one thing
And possess another;
For this alone can deeply hinder
An unsaved sister or a brother.

You Are Not Forgotten

I know right now ~ things may seem blue,
Be of good cheer He has not ~ forgotten you.

He chose you to preach ~ and to teach as well.
There is no way ~ the church will fail.
When you were chosen ~ to work on land;
failure was never ever ~ A part of God's plan.

He sees the hurt you feel within,
fret not, because it will soon;
come to an end.

Be encouraged my Pastor,
you have not been forgotten,
by our dear and loving Master.

Somebody Cares

Somebody knows when your heart aches,
and everything seem to go wrong;
Somebody knows when your shadows need,
chasing with a song

Somebody knows when your are lonely
Tired, discouraged and blue;
Somebody wants you to know Him
And that He dearly loves you.

Somebody knows when you are tempted
And your mind has grown dizzy and dim;
Somebody cares when you are at your weakest
and farthest away from Him.

Somebody grieves when you are falling
You are never lost from His sight;
Somebody waits for your coming,
and He'll drive the gloom from the night.

Somebody loves you ~ when you are weary
Somebody loves you when you're strong;
Somebody's waiting to help you,
He watches from the throne.

Needing His friendship so Holy
Needing His watchful care so true;
His name, we call Him Jesus
He loves everyone including YOU.

He's There For You

If you seek direction,
from the Creator of man;
You can become someone great,
if you really believe you can.

Tell Him your desires,
and all that you want to do;
Remain steadfast until,
He has spoken directly to you.

His judgment is right
and He's perfect too;
He knows exactly,
what is best for you.

Don't give up,
don't go astray;
He just may lead you,
to go a different way.

Give Him your all,
in whatsoever you do.
As long as you try,
He will be there for you.

You've Got A Friend

When the life of a loved one
Comes to an end,
That is the time,
You really need a friend.

They will hold your hand,
and walk by your side.
While you release the hurt,
you are feeling inside.

God is your friend,
He is there for you;
For He know's exactly where you are,
and what you are going through.

The tragedy of death,
God truly knows.
For He experienced the death of His son,
a long time ago.

Don't Give Up

The coming of the Lord,
is not far away;
So I say to the saint's,
let us not give up today.

Not because tomorrow,
all will be well;
But because today we serve a God,
who cannot fail.

No matter what we see,
sense or feel;
It wouldn't be happening
if it wasn't in God's will.

Our lives would be more,
full of joy than sorrow.
If only we would forget yesterday,
live today and trust Him for tomorrow.

Think

Think like a winner
So you won't ever sink;
What really determines this
Is how you really think.

Stay focused and think positive
When there are distractions;
Remember, how you think
Is shown in your actions.

Thinking this way
You can't go wrong;
You'll become that winner
If you stand firm and stand strong.

Understanding, Wisdom and Knowledge

Understanding others
You must try and do;
But before that,
take time to fully understand you.

Wisdom is the greatest,
in all that you know;
It is ever so needed,
everywhere you go.

Knowledge helps you,
make decisions that's right;
It helps you to yield,
when your flesh wants' to fight.

Better Ambition

Some people say ambition is good
Others say, it's bad;
But if we lived without it
The world would be sad.

I's good to have ambition
And walk upright;
For it will help you achieve
Goals beyond sight.

It's okay to be content
While others are being blessed.
But lacking ambition
You can't be your best.

Parents want their children to have
Better than what they had;
Of that which was good,
And none of the bad.

A better home, job
Education and car;
But it takes ambiton
To get them thus far.

If Possible

If possible, I'd give my fellow man
Never a reason to cry;
And if possible, I'd give every soldier
Never a cause to die.

If possible, I'd cleanse the world
Of all its fear and pain;
And if possible, I'd take away
Every cause for shame.

If possible, I'd make the sun
Shine most every day;
And if possible, every hurt child's tears
I would kiss away.

If possible, I'd insure that lovers
Would never have a fight;
And if possible, I'd give everyone
Someone to hold ~ close each night.

If possible, I'd guarantee Heaven
And do away with Hell;
And if possible, I'd give to every broken spirit
To be whole and to be well.

If This Is the End

If you want to leave
Please feel free;
Don't pressure yourself,
to stay with Me.

Before you leave
Let this be understood;
Once you are gone
you will be gone for good.

I love you dearly,
And this you know;
but if you choose freedom,
I must let you go.

Please don't look back
When you head for the door;
Because if you do
it will hurt me even the more.

Don't stop to explain
Don't tell me why;
If this is really the end,
Just bid me farewell and goodbye.

To everyone, thank you and I pray something within these pages help, healed or inspired you!

- **Mamie**

CPSIA information can be obtained
at www.ICGtesting.com
Printed in the USA
LVHW100926090922
727941LV00001B/251